Native Americans

Shoshone

Barbara A. Gray-Kanatiiosh

ABDO Publishing Company

visit us at
www.abdopub.com

Published by ABDO Publishing Company, 4940 Viking Drive, Suite 622, Edina, Minnesota 55435. Copyright © 2004 by Abdo Consulting Group, Inc. International copyrights reserved in all countries. No part of this book may be reproduced in any form without written permission from the publisher.

Printed in the United States.

Cover Photo: Corbis
Interior Photos: Corbis pp. 4, 28, 29, 30
Illustrations: David Kanietakeron Fadden pp. 7, 9, 11, 13, 15, 17, 19, 21, 23, 25, 27
Editors: Kate A. Conley, Jennifer R. Krueger, Kristin Van Cleaf
Art Direction & Maps: Neil Klinepier

Library of Congress Cataloging-in-Publication Data

Gray-Kanatiiosh, Barbara A., 1963-
   Shoshone / Barbara A. Gray-Kanatiiosh.
    p. cm. -- (Native Americans. Set III)
   Includes bibliographical references and index.
   Summary: An introduction to the history, social structure, customs, and present life of the Shoshone Indians.
   ISBN 1-57765-939-2
   1. Shoshoni Indians--History--Juvenile literature. 2. Shoshoni Indians--Social life and customs--Juvenile literature. [1. Shoshoni Indians. 2. Indians of North America--West (U.S.)] I. Title. II. Native Americans (Edina, Minn.). Set III

E99.S4G73 2003
978.004'9745--dc21

2003042586

About the Author: Barbara A. Gray-Kanatiiosh, JD

Barbara Gray-Kanatiiosh, JD, Ph.D. ABD, is an Akwesasne Mohawk. She resides at the Mohawk Nation and is of the Wolf Clan. She has a Juris Doctorate from Arizona State University, where she was one of the first recipients of ASU's special certificate in Indian Law. Barbara's Ph.D. is in Justice Studies at ASU. She is currently working on her dissertation, which concerns the impacts of environmental injustice on indigenous culture. Barbara works hard to educate children about Native Americans through her writing and Web site, where children may ask questions and receive a written response about the Haudenosaunee culture. The Web site is: www.peace4turtleisland.org

About the Illustrator: David Kanietakeron Fadden

David Kanietakeron Fadden is a member of the Akwesasne Mohawk Wolf Clan. His work has appeared in publications such as *Akwesasne Notes*, *Indian Time*, and the *Northeast Indian Quarterly*. Examples of his work have also appeared in various publications of the Six Nations Indian Museum in Onchiota, NY. His work has also appeared in "How the West Was Lost: Always the Enemy," produced by Gannett Production, which appeared on the Discovery Channel. David's work has been exhibited in Albany, NY; the Lake Placid Center for the Arts; Centre Strathearn in Montreal, Quebec; North Country Community College in Saranac Lake, NY; Paul Smith's College in Paul Smiths, NY; and at the Unison Arts & Learning Center in New Paltz, NY.

Contents

Where They Lived

The Shoshone (shuh-SHOHN) called themselves *Newe* or *Nimi*. This name means "the people" in their language. The Shoshone language is part of the Numic branch of the Uto-Aztecan language family.

The Shoshone homelands included parts of present-day Wyoming, Montana, Utah, Idaho, California, and Nevada. Neighboring tribes included the Bannock, Paiute, Crow, Cheyenne, Lakota, and Arapaho.

The Snake River in Wyoming

The Shoshone lived west of the Bighorn Mountains and east of the Snake River. Their territory stretched northward to present-day Montana. To the south, Shoshone territory reached the Uinta Mountains and the Green River. Some western Shoshone territory reached present-day southeastern California.

4

Shoshone homelands contained plains, basins, canyons, valleys, and mountains. There were also lakes, streams, ponds, marshes, rivers, and even deserts. These areas were home to many types of fish, birds, and animals. Trees, shrubs, berries, wildflowers, and other plants grew on the land.

Shoshone Homelands

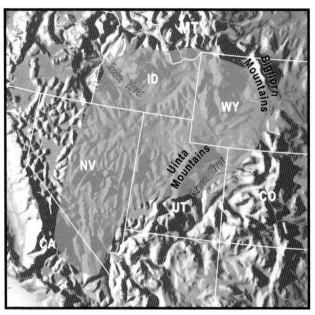

Society

The Shoshone lived in bands made up of extended families. Each band was named after its leader or after a river near the band's settlement.

Shoshone bands were **seminomadic**. They followed the **migrating** animals and the ripening of wild plants. They made seasonal rounds to gather, hunt, and fish.

Each band had a leader. The leader, or chief, led by the agreement of everyone and not by force. Shoshone society had other leaders, too. A war leader made sure that the people were protected from enemies. Spiritual leaders' lives centered on religion.

The Shoshone also had medicine people who interpreted dreams and aided in **vision quests**. They offered thanks to the Creator for plants and animals, which the Shoshone needed to survive. Medicine people also healed with **rituals** and herbs. And, they conducted annual ceremonies.

A medicine man
interprets a dream.

Food

The Shoshone hunted, fished, and gathered their food. The men caught small animals in snares and traps. They used bows and arrows, lances, and knives to hunt larger animals. These animals included elks, pronghorn, bighorn sheep, deer, and bison.

Hunting bison was especially dangerous work. The hunters moved close to the bison. They cut its legs to slow it down. Then, the men could kill it with a lance or bow and arrow.

Men also fished for salmon, trout, and other fish. They used hook and line, nets, and spears to catch the fish. Men also caught fish by building a **weir** or a dam. Fish swam into the weir and were easily caught.

Shoshone women also collected food for the family. They gathered wild vegetables, fruits, seeds, piñon nuts, berries, and **camas** roots. The women roasted the camas roots in a fire pit. They ground the cooked roots into **meal** and made it into mush or bread.

The Shoshone dried some of this food for the winter. They prepared food such as fish by cutting it into strips and drying the strips on racks. They also smoked meat to preserve it. Sometimes the Shoshone stored their preserved food in caves.

The Shoshone were thankful for their food. They performed first ceremonies to give thanks to the plants, fish, and animals they depended on for survival. For example, a circle dance was held for the first salmon caught.

Shoshone men hunting a bison

Homes

The Shoshone lived in different kinds of homes. Winter homes were permanent. The Shoshone built these homes along large rivers. The rivers provided food, water, and an escape route. Seasonal homes were temporary. The Shoshone could easily move them from place to place.

During seasonal travel, the Shoshone slept in brush shelters. They also made temporary shelters by stretching animal hides over a few poles to make a lean-to. Sometimes, they even slept in caves.

During the winter, the Shoshone lived in cone-shaped tepees. They formed a tepee frame with sapling poles. They tied the poles at the top with cord or **rawhide**. Then they covered the frame with slabs of bark, grass, or animal hides. A hole at the top of the tepee let out smoke.

Sometimes, people piled stones along the outside of the tepee to anchor it and also to block the wind. They entered and exited

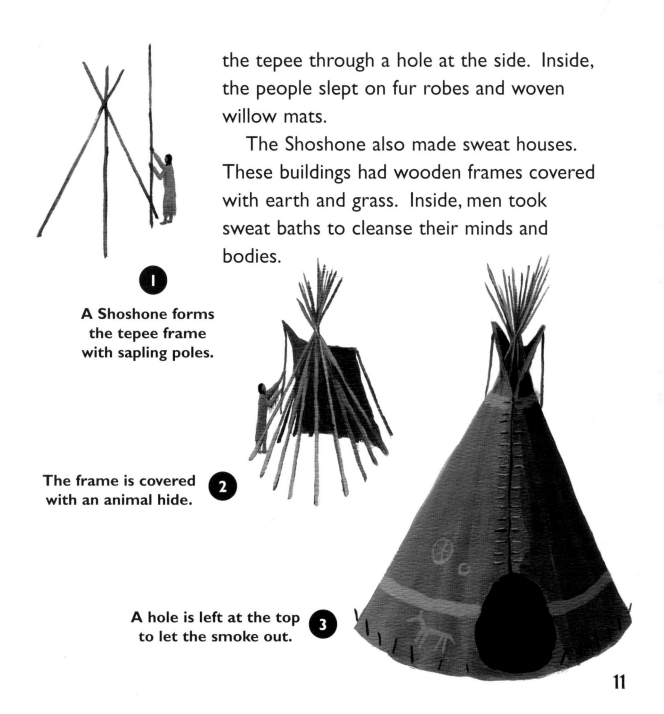

the tepee through a hole at the side. Inside, the people slept on fur robes and woven willow mats.

The Shoshone also made sweat houses. These buildings had wooden frames covered with earth and grass. Inside, men took sweat baths to cleanse their minds and bodies.

1 A Shoshone forms the tepee frame with sapling poles.

2 The frame is covered with an animal hide.

3 A hole is left at the top to let the smoke out.

11

Clothing

The Shoshone made clothing from bison, deer, pronghorn, and elk hides. They decorated their clothing with floral designs. To do this, they used materials such as porcupine quills, bones, hooves, and **ermine** tails. Later, the Shoshone began trading for glass seed beads. Then the women began using a combination of quills and beads.

Shoshone women wore fringed dresses. They decorated each dress with shells, horns, and elk teeth. Women also wore short leggings.

Men wore shirts with tight-fitting, fringed sleeves. The Shoshone often made a shirt from a single animal hide that hung down to the man's thigh. The men also wore **breechcloths** and leggings. The leggings protected their legs from brush and thorns.

Shoshone men also wore headdresses. Traditionally, a man earned one eagle feather for each brave deed. So, a large eagle feather headdress meant a man was courageous and respected.

Both men and women wore robes. They used fur robes in the winter and hairless robes in the summer. The Shoshone also wore moccasins that had a seam on their outside edges. The top of each moccasin was decorated with a floral pattern of porcupine quills.

The Shoshone sometimes wore beautiful cowls, too. A cowl covered a person's neck, chest, and belly. An otter **pelt** formed the collar. Strips of **ermine** fur hung from the collar.

Traditional Shoshone clothing

Crafts

Shoshone women created beautiful porcupine **quillwork**. They used quillwork to decorate shirts, dresses, leggings, armbands, bags, moccasins, and other clothing. Women often gathered in quillwork circles for this. They shared stories and taught the younger women how to quill.

To begin a quillwork project, women pulled quills from a porcupine hide. They cleaned the quills and sorted them according to size. Then, they dyed the quills. Dyes were made from wild onion skins, wild berries, and plant roots.

Quills were hard when dry. So, a woman would put a quill in her mouth to soften it. Then she would bite down on the quill to flatten it. After this task was completed, the quills were ready to use.

Opposite page: Shoshone women in a quillwork circle discuss the decoration on a moccasin.

Next, women would sew the quills onto clothing. They used bone needles and **awls**, as well as thread made from bison **sinew**. A Shoshone woman often wore an awl around her neck. The awl's case was made out of heavy leather and decorated with **quillwork**.

Family

Every family member was expected to contribute to the survival of the Shoshone band. Men, women, children, and elders all had their own responsibilities.

Men made tools for hunting and fishing. They carved bows from juniper wood, and then rubbed each bow with **tallow**. Next, they wrapped thin strips of **sinew** around the bow. This strengthened the bow and also made it waterproof. The Shoshone made the bowstring out of hemp fibers.

The women skillfully prepared fish and hides. They used scrapers to cut away the meat and hair from the hides. They **tanned** the leather with the animal's brains. Tanning softened the leather and prepared it for making clothing.

The Shoshone elders had responsibilities, too. They made horns and hooves into glue. The Shoshone also made bison horns into tools, cups, and bowls.

Opposite page: A Shoshone woman prepares an animal hide.

Children

The Shoshone loved and cared for their children. Parents carried their babies on willow **cradleboards**. Cradleboards kept babies safe and happy.

Older Shoshone children helped with daily chores, such as gathering wild berries, seeds, or vegetables. The children also helped gather pine nuts. To do this, they used a long stick to knock pinecones from the trees. Then, they gathered the pinecones and removed the pine nuts.

Shoshone children also learned from their elders. Elders taught children ceremonial songs and dances. They told children the stories of their people. Elders also taught children how to make four-holed flutes, bone whistles, and musical bows. These instruments were played during ceremonies.

Shoshone children also had time to run, swim, and play games. For instance, they played with whip tops. A whip top was about three inches (8 cm) tall and was carved from bone, wood, or stone.

The children used leather thongs tied to one end of a long stick to whip the top. Each player tried to keep his or her top twirling longer than the other players' tops.

Children also played with stilts. Stilts were made from two tree branches with limbs that forked. Children wrapped willow where the limb forked. This created a place for the foot to rest.

An elder teaches Shoshone children by telling them stories.

Myths

Native American nations often have stories that tell how people came to this world. The following is one version of a Shoshone creation story.

A long time ago Wolf created humans. Wolf placed them inside a willow jug basket. This jug basket was woven so tightly that it could hold water.

Wolf gave his brother Coyote a simple job. Wolf said, "Do not open the jug until you get to the Great Basin." Coyote said, "I can do that." Coyote carried the willow jug in his mouth.

When Coyote was on the east coast of North America, he heard drumming and singing. It was coming from inside the jug. Coyote, being curious, opened the jug. As soon as the jug opened, the humans ran out. They ran all over North and South America.

By the time Coyote got the jug closed, only a pair of humans remained inside. Coyote finally reached his destination. He opened the jug and out fell the pair. They became known as the Shoshone.

Coyote opens the
jug too soon.

21

War

Before the Shoshone had contact with Europeans, war rarely happened. Fights only occurred when hostile tribes entered Shoshone lands. When the Shoshone did need to fight, they were prepared with many different weapons.

Weapons of war were the same as hunting weapons for the Shoshone. They fought with bows and arrows, knives, and lances. They used an elk horn to sharpen knives and arrowhead points.

The warriors also used a club for fighting at close range. This weapon had a long handle covered with leather. Attached to the handle was a two-pound (1-kg) rock also covered in leather. When a warrior swung the club, the rock hit the target hard.

The Shoshone wore bone breastplates and chokers for protection. It was hard for an arrow, knife, or lance to pierce these bone plates. Warriors also made **rawhide** shields. They used bison rawhide because it was strong.

Warriors sometimes painted designs on their shields. The designs often came from a vision. Warriors believed the design and their spirit guides would protect them in battle.

A Shoshone man is prepared for battle with breastplate, choker, and shield.

Contact with Europeans

Through trade with Europeans, the Shoshone obtained horses. Horses made hunting large animals, such as bison, much easier. However, horses also brought problems. Fighting between the Shoshone and other tribes increased after horses were introduced.

Though the Shoshone traded successfully for horses, they could not trade for everything they wanted. Neighboring tribes had traded with the French for guns. The Shoshone wanted guns, too. But, they were unable to obtain them.

Not having guns put the Shoshone at a disadvantage. Tribes attacking with guns forced some Shoshone off their traditional lands. Shoshone men spent their time protecting women and children from raids.

In 1805, the Shoshone came in contact with a group of American explorers. The Lewis and Clark Expedition met the Lemhi band of Shoshone. The expedition was looking for a route to the Pacific Ocean. Sacagawea, a Shoshone woman, helped guide the men.

Over time, white settlers and miners began flooding into Shoshone territory. The Shoshone fought against this. In 1863, about 200 Shoshone were killed along the Bear River by volunteer soldiers. Many Shoshone also died from diseases such as smallpox.

The Shoshone faced more problems in 1887. That year, the U.S. Congress passed the Dawes General Allotment Act. It encouraged Native Americans to own land individually. However, individual land ownership was not the traditional way of Shoshone society. This law put traditional Shoshone culture in danger.

Sacagawea guides Lewis and Clark.

Washakie

Washakie (wahsh'-uh-kee) was a respected Shoshone leader, orator, and peacekeeper. The name *Washakie* means "**Rawhide Rattle.**" Washakie received his name after making a rawhide rattle from the first bison he killed. Washakie shook the rattle during raids and battles to scare the horses of his enemies.

No one knows exactly when Washakie was born. But by 1850, he had become principal chief of the Eastern Shoshone. Washakie wanted to protect his people and maintain peace. He believed negotiating with the United States, rather than fighting, was the best way to protect his people.

Washakie worked as a scout for General George Cook of the U.S. Army. In 1868, Washakie negotiated a peace treaty that created the Wind River Reservation. He helped the settlers have safe passage.

In later years, Washakie grew unhappy with the United States. The Shoshone had been promised supplies, seeds, animals, and tools. But the U.S. government did not uphold these treaty promises.

Washakie died in 1900. The U.S. government gave him a full military funeral and burial. This honored Washakie's career in the U.S. Army.

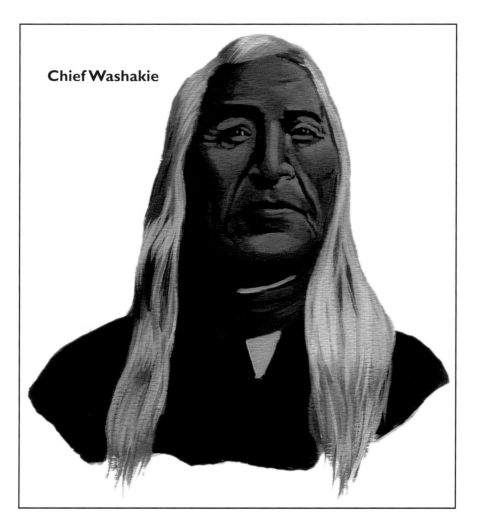

Chief Washakie

The Shoshone Today

Today, there are an estimated 10,000 Shoshone tribal members. They have 14 **federally recognized** Shoshone reservations. These reservations are located in Utah, California, Wyoming, Idaho, and Nevada.

The Shoshone share their reservations with other tribes. Some of the reservations include the Shoshone-Bannock Tribes of the Fort Hall Reservation, the Shoshone Tribe of the Wind River Reservation, and the Shoshone-Paiute Tribes of the Duck Valley Reservation.

The Sacagawea dollar coin

In 2000, the United States introduced the Sacagawea dollar coin. The coin was made to honor the Shoshone for helping the Lewis and Clark Expedition of 1804–1806. Today, both Sacagawea and Chief Washakie are buried at the Wind River Reservation in Wyoming.

The Shoshone are working hard to restore their language and culture. They hold traditional ceremonies such as the sun dance, bear dance, and round dance. These ceremonies consist of dancing, singing, and offering thanks.

Traditionally dressed girls at the Wind River Indian Reservation in Wyoming

A Shoshone dances at the Wind River Reservation.

Glossary

awl - a pointed tool for making small holes in materials, such as leather or wood.

breechcloth - a piece of hide or cloth, usually worn by men, that wraps between the legs and ties with a belt around the waist.

camas - a plant that is found mostly in the western United States and is safe to eat.

cradleboard - a flat board used to hold a baby. It could be carried on the mother's back or hung from a tree so that the baby could see what was going on.

ermine - a weasel with a white coat.

federal recognition - the U.S. government's recognition of a tribe as being an independent nation. The tribe is then eligible for special funding and for protection of its reservation lands.

meal - coarsely ground seeds.

migrate - to move from one place to settle in another.

pelt - an animal skin with the fur still on it.

quillwork - the use of porcupine quills to make designs on clothing or cradleboards.

rawhide - untanned cattle hide.

ritual - a form or order to a ceremony.

seminomad - a member of a people that moves from place to place, but has a home base where homes are built and crops are grown.

sinew - a band of tough fibers that joins a muscle to a bone.

tallow - the melted fat of cattle and sheep used in making candles and soap.

tan - to make a hide into leather by soaking it in a special liquid.

vision quest - a way for Native Americans, especially young people, to communicate with nature and the spirit world. People on vision quests seek advice, answers to questions, and an understanding of why they have come to the earth.

weir - a trap set in water to catch fish.

Web Sites

To learn more about the Shoshone, visit ABDO Publishing Company on the World Wide Web at **www.abdopub.com**. Web sites about the Shoshone are featured on our Book Links page. These links are routinely monitored and updated to provide the most current information available.

Index